By Laura Williams
Translated by Emma Svensson

© 2022 Williams Books
1 rue de l'église, 91430 Igny
Dépôt légal : Décembre 2022
ISBN 978-2-494614-53-6
Imprimé à la demande par Amazon
Loi n° 49-956 du 16 juillet 1949 sur les publications destinées à la jeunesse

antilop

antelope

fladdermus

bat

björn
bear

vägglöss
bedbug

bi
bee

buffel
buffalo

fjäril
butterfly

kamel
camel

katt

cat

kameleont

chameleon

brud
chick

kyckling
chicken

kackerlacka

cockroach

ko

cow

syrsa
cricket

krokodil
crocodile

hund

dog

åsna

donkey

anka

duck

daggmask

earthworm

elefant

elephant

fisk

fish

fluga

fly

räv

fox

groda
frog

gasell
gazelle

giraff
giraffe

get
goat

gås
goose

flodhäst
hipopotamus

häst

horse

hyena

hyena

lejon

lion

ödla

lizard

mullvad

mole

mungo

mongoose

apa
monkey

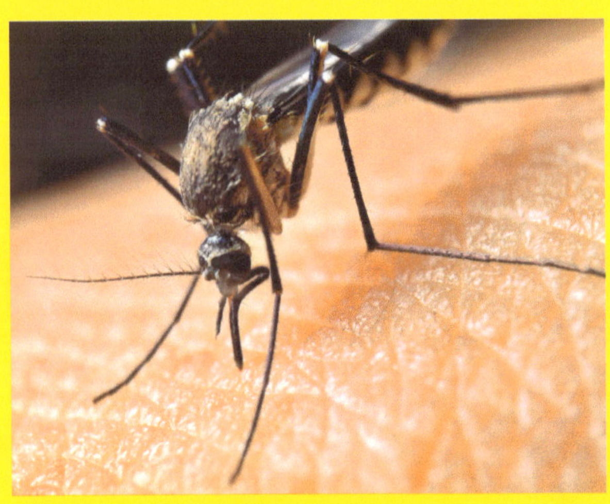

mygga
mosquito

mus

mouse

papegoja

parrot

gris

pig

duva

pigeon

kanin

rabbit

tupp

rooster

får
sheep

snigel
snail

orm
snake

spindel
spider

geting
wasp

zebra
zebra

Thank you

Thank you for purchasing "Swedish-English Words for Toddlers"! Your support means a lot to me, and I hope you and your child enjoy these books.

If you have a moment, I would greatly appreciate it if you could leave a review on Amazon. Your feedback will help me improve future editions of the series and create more resources for bilingual children.

Thank you again for your support. You can access the reviews on Amazon by scanning the QR code below or by visiting the link below:

https://www.amazon.com/review/create-review?&asin=2494614538

Thank you for helping me continue my work as a language teacher and translator. Your support is greatly appreciated!

In the same collection

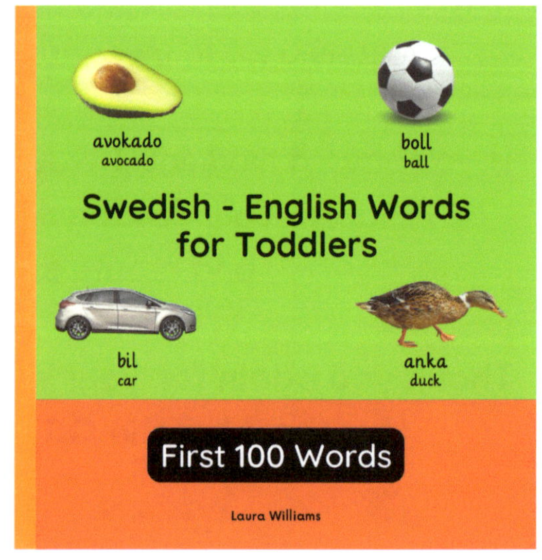